SCRUMPTIOUS & SUSTAINABLE
FISHCAKES

D1613885

SCRUMPTIOUS & SUSTAINABLE
FISHCAKES

A Collection of the Best Sustainable Fishcake Recipes
from Canadian Chefs, Coast to Coast

With Recipes By
Elizabeth Feltham, Elaine Elliot, Craig Flinn, Virginia Lee,
Sandra Nowlan and Maureen Tilley

Compiled by the Formac Cookbook Team

FORMAC PUBLISHING COMPANY LIMITED
HALIFAX

ACKOWLEDGEMENTS

Recipes in this book come from *Fabulous Fishcakes* by Elizabeth Feltham, with exceptions from the following sources: *Low-Salt Dash Dinners* by Sandra Nowlan, 17; *Hold that Hidden Salt!* by Maureen Tilley, 19; *Lobster* by Elaine Elliot and Virginia Lee, 54; *Pacific Flavours* by Virginia Lee, 56; *Fresh & Local* by Craig Flinn, 80; *Fresh Canadian Bistro* by Craig Flinn, 84; *Fresh & Frugal* by Craig Flinn, 90.

Copyright © 2011 Formac Publishing Company Limited

All rights reserved. No part of this book may be reproduced or transmitted in any form or by any means, electronic or mechanical, including photocopying, or by any information storage or retrieval system, without permission in writing from the publisher.

Formac Publishing Company Limited recognizes the support of the Province of Nova Scotia through the Department of Tourism, Culture and Heritage. We acknowledge the financial support of the Government of Canada through the Canada Book Fund for our publishing activities.

NOVA SCOTIA
NOUVELLE-ÉCOSSE
Tourism, Culture and Heritage
Tourisme, Culture et Patrimoine

The Canada Council | Le Conseil des Arts
for the Arts | du Canada

Library and Archives Canada Cataloguing in Publication

Scrumptious & sustainable fishcakes : a collection of the best sustainable fishcake recipes from Canadian chefs, coast to coast / with recipes by Elizabeth Feltham ... [et al.] ; compiled by the Formac Cookbook Team.

Issued also in electronic format.
ISBN 978-0-88780-983-5

1. Fish cakes. 2. Cooking (Fish). 3. Cookbooks. I. Feltham, Elizabeth II. Formac Cookbook Team III. Title: Scrumptious and sustainable fishcakes.

TX747.S37 2011   641.6'92   C2011-904210-X

Formac Publishing Company Limited
5502 Atlantic Street
Halifax, Nova Scotia, Canada
B3H 1G4
www.formac.ca

Printed and bound in China.

CONTENTS

Look for these sustainability symbols for each species featured in the book to help you make good choices. See the introduction for all of the details, and the chapter opener pages for more species-related information.

 BEST CHOICE

 SOME CONCERNS

 AVOID

INTRODUCTION

The success of *Fabulous Fishcakes* shows that people are interested in creative fishcake recipes, and with growing environmental concerns people are becoming more aware of the importance of sustainable selections. So we have put this collection together with a strong sustainability orientation.

Canada's oceans are an important source of food for Canadians, and wild fisheries and aquaculture are both important parts of our coastal economies. From the east coast to the west coast, from the northern Arctic waters to the Great Lakes, all manner of molluscs, crustaceans and fish are available for our gastronomic delight.

Seafood has long been a key asset of our nation, both culturally and economically. However, with the collapse of the cod fishery in the early 1990s, we, along with the rest of the world, were forced to face some hard realities: seafood stocks are not infinite, and the fishing industry cannot operate as if they are. Since then, the government has brought down tougher regulations on fishing practices, and various environmental organizations have taken on the task of monitoring the sustainability of Canada's fisheries.

As consumers and as citizens we have real power to ensure the future of our seafood bounty. We can choose and purchase fish in an environmentally responsible way to make sure our children and grandchildren can enjoy the same delicious tastes and textures we do today. This is what sustainability means, in a nutshell. To shop and eat sustainably is to support food practices that are ultimately better for the environment and deliver a higher-quality product to our dinner tables.

In addition to supporting the preservation and protection of our ecosystem, the sustainability movement goes hand in hand with the current "eat local" movement that is gaining popularity and strengthening consumers' contact with their local farmers and community agriculture. Choosing seafood that is found in waters closest to us helps to put us more in tune with our local fisheries and to better observe the status and safety of specific species. We also benefit from fresher-tasting fish and a healthier local fishing industry.

Choosing sustainable options has never been easier. Currently, there are many organizations monitoring fishing practices and assessing and certifying the best varieties for consumption. By choosing seafood conscientiously, we can preserve not only the harvested species, but restore and maintain the oceans' ecological balance as a whole. Making sustainable choices in purchasing fish and seafood is a wonderful way to better the environment, strengthen our local communities and industry and satisfy our taste buds.

We have a role as citizens as well. We can push for governments to shift the balance in their decisions and policies about the fishery. It was, after all, a failure of government policy that generated the collapse of the Atlantic cod fishery. It is the failure of policy that threatens Pacific salmon, so much so that finally a government inquiry was called. As consumers we can play a role by making smart purchasing choices; as citizens we can insist that fishery policies be built on sustainability, not the desires of the fishing industry.

MAKING BETTER CHOICES

There are many variables to consider when shopping for sustainable seafood, and it can be difficult to sift through the wealth of information and advice on the subject. SeaChoice is a Canadian organization that has developed a simple ranking system to aid consumers in finding the best sustainable option for any type of seafood. Formed jointly by the Canadian Parks and Wilderness Society, the David Suzuki Foundation, Ecology Action Center, Living Oceans Society and the Sierra Club British Columbia, SeaChoice is a comprehensive organization committed to supporting healthy oceans, and in particular to helping Canadian consumers make better choices about their seafood consumption.

SeaChoice utilizes science-based assessment methods developed by the Monterey Bay Aquarium's Seafood Watch Program when determining the sustainability of a particular species and, based on this, labels them under one of three categories: Best Choice, Some Concerns, or Avoid. Fish labelled Best Choice come from abundant, healthy species that are harvested in an environmentally sustainable way. Seafood labelled Some Concerns have been determined to have certain issues with the management or impact of that fishery; these species should be consumed infrequently or only when a Best Choice species is unavailable. Seafood varieties in the Avoid category are those that are affected by many problems, and could be endangered or harvested in an environmentally irresponsible manner.

When ranking seafood in these categories, SeaChoice looks at five main criteria:

- Inherent vulnerability to fishing pressure
- Status of wild stocks
- Nature and extent of discarded bycatch (fish caught unintentionally in fishery)
- Effect of fishing practices on habitats and ecosystems
- Effectiveness of the management regime

On a case-by-case basis, SeaChoice applies each of these assessments to a seafood species, taking into account how the species was caught and its geographical location.

The Seafood Guide card published by SeaChoice compiles this information in an easy-to-read format that you can use as a quick reference when shopping for seafood. SeaChoice standards are continually reassessed, so the most up-to-date information is found on their website: www.seachoice.org/

In addition to SeaChoice, the Marine Stewardship Council (MSC) also provides valuable information about sustainable seafood choices and carries out an international ecolabelling program. The MSC is an independent non-profit organization with an ecolabel and fishery certification program. Founded in 1997 by the World Wide Fund for Nature and Unilever, a giant food multinational, MSC became an independent program in 1999. MSC has developed standards for fisheries, and often places conditions on a fishery that it must achieve to maintain certification. SeaChoice rankings are based on the current practices in use, and not on projected improvements to the fishery practices. The MSC has two standards, one for sustainable fishing

and another for seafood traceability, meaning the chain of custody through which the seafood passes. Fisheries and seafood businesses voluntarily seek certification by third parties that they are following the relevant standards to meet the world's "best practice" guidelines for certification and ecolabelling.

The MSC standard considers the following in certifying a fishery sustainable:

- *Sustainable fish stocks*: Fishing level must be sustainable for the population of the species, not overexploiting the resource.
- *Minimizing environmental impact*: The fishing operation must not interfere with the ecosystem on which the fishery depends.
- *Effective management*: The fishery must meet all laws (local, national and international) and respond to changing circumstances to maintain sustainability.

MSC's chain of custody standard for seafood traceability ensures that fish sold with the MSC ecolabel comes from a certified sustainable fishery, and that all companies in the supply chain, from boat to plate, have the certification. This keeps illegally caught seafood out of the supply chain and promotes traceability.

There are cases where species are MSC certified as sustainable and labelled as Avoid or Some Concerns by SeaChoice. This is because SeaChoice rankings are based on a current assessment of the fishery, whereas MSC certifies but places conditions that the fishery must meet over a period of time. In other cases, SeaChoice is more specific (for example deeming that hook-and-line fishing for haddock is less damaging than bottom trawl, whereas MSC certifies the entire fishery with different conditions on trawl, gillnet and longline, depending on the level of ecosystem damage). SeaChoice evaluates the different types of gear used in a fishery – for example bottom trawls versus bottom longlines, troll versus

SALMON

The rich, buttery flavour of salmon is indicative of its high oil content. Any of the salmon types, fresh or frozen, will yield excellent fishcakes. When buying whole fish, look for shiny scales and bright eyes. If the fish is already filleted, check for smell — there shouldn't be a strong fishy aroma. When buying frozen, beware of signs of freezer burn or frost in the package. Canned salmon is not recommended for these recipes, but could be experimented with in a pinch.

There are five species of Pacific salmon, most still wild caught, which are sold under the market names of sockeye, chinook, chum, coho or pink salmon. Wild BC salmon are partially certified by the Marine Stewardship Council (MSC) and categorized as Some Concerns by SeaChoice. These are a better choice than farmed salmon because they are low in contaminants and come from a well-managed fishery. The statuses of individual stocks of Pacific salmon vary considerably from year to year, and the concerns from SeaChoice arise from low stocks of certain species in 2010.

Different species of Pacific salmon have unique flavours and textures. Chinook salmon has high oil content and a rich flavour, and takes a rub or marinade well. Sockeye has a strong wild flavour and should be used with other strong flavours. Coho has a firm texture. Pink is mostly used for canned salmon or pet food.

Almost all commercially viable Atlantic salmon is now farmed and, as a result, is associated with environmental concerns and health risks due to high levels of contaminants. Farmed salmon are assessed as a species to avoid by SeaChoice. The problem with farmed salmon comes largely from the fact that they are raised in net pens in both the Atlantic and Pacific oceans. This increases the risk of escapes to wild stocks, pollution, disease and parasite transfer and puts a strain on marine resources. There is no MSC label for farmed salmon because they do not certify aquaculture species at the present time. In the future, there will be more of a push for closed containment for farming.

For more information on SeaChoice rankings and MSC certification, please refer to the introduction on page 6.

SALMON AND WASABI FISHCAKES

Charlotte Lane Café, Shelburne, NS

"Even though it's not a traditional Maritime dish," says Kathleen Glauser, "this dish has gathered a real local following, especially with our Saturday brunch customers." She suggests serving it with a green salad.

8 oz (225 g) salmon, skinless and boned
½ tsp (2 mL) olive oil
½ cup (125 mL) chopped red onions
1 tbsp (15 mL) chopped garlic
1 cup (250 mL) mashed potatoes (½ lb / 225 g)
1 tbsp (15 mL) Worcestershire sauce
½ tsp (2 mL) dried dill
1 tsp (5 mL) salt
½ tsp (2 mL) pepper
1 tsp (5 mL) paprika
2 tsp (10 mL) wasabi powder
For breading:
½ to 1 cup (125 to 250 mL) flour
For cooking:
olive oil

Bring a saucepan or deep skillet of water to boil; turn heat to medium and place salmon in pan, ensuring water covers fish. Cook until salmon flakes apart easily, drain and let cool.

In a frying pan, heat olive oil, sauté red onions and garlic until soft, remove from heat.

In a large bowl, combine salmon, potatoes, red onions, garlic, Worcestershire sauce, dill, salt, pepper, paprika and wasabi.

Form into patties and refrigerate for several hours.

Dust with flour.

Fry in olive oil over medium heat until browned on both sides, turning once.

4 fishcakes / 2 servings

Suggested sauce: Curry Mango Mayonnaise (see page 21)

CORNMEAL-CRUSTED SALMON CAKES WITH APRICOT AND CURRANT CHUTNEY

Windsor House, St. Andrews-by-the-Sea, NB

Chef Peter Woodworth has created exotically seasoned salmon cakes that not only have excellent flavour, but also are versatile. They make an elegant brunch dish, accompanied by Apricot and Currant Chutney, but we also enjoy them in an informal setting served on whole-wheat buns topped with lettuce, onion, tomato, Dijon mustard and Yogurt and Caper Dressing.

1 lb (500 g) fresh salmon fillet, cut in several
    pieces
4 tbsp (60 mL) chopped green onions
1 clove garlic, minced
2 egg whites
¼ tsp (1 mL) freshly ground pepper
4 tbsp (60 mL) soft breadcrumbs
⅔ cup (150 mL) cornmeal
1 tbsp (15 mL) cumin
1 tsp (5 mL) cayenne pepper
½ tsp (2 mL) cinnamon
2 tbsp (30 mL) finely chopped fresh tarragon
4 tsp (20 mL) olive oil
For serving:
crisp greens
steamed asparagus

Combine salmon, green onions, garlic, egg whites, pepper and breadcrumbs in a food processor. Pulse a few times until salmon is coarsely chopped.

Rinse your hands with cold water and form the salmon mixture into 6 patties. Refrigerate several hours or overnight to help keep shape when cooking.

On a piece of waxed paper, combine cornmeal, cumin, cayenne, cinnamon and tarragon. Gently press into the patties.

Place a non-stick pan over medium heat, add olive oil and transfer patties to the pan with a spatula. Sauté until golden brown, turning very carefully only once.

Serve salmon cakes with crisp greens, steamed asparagus and Apricot and Currant Chutney or Yogurt and Caper Dressing.

6 salmon cakes / 6 servings

Suggested sauce: Apricot and Currant Chutney or Yogurt and Caper Dressing

Apricot and Currant Chutney

1 cup (250 mL) diced sun-dried apricots
⅔ cup (150 mL) chopped sweet onion or shallots
2 cloves garlic, minced
1 cup (250 mL) white wine
½ cup (125 mL) water
1 tbsp (15 mL) honey
½ cup (125 mL) white wine vinegar or cider
    vinegar
¼ cup (60 mL) dried currants
2 tbsp (30 mL) sliced almonds

Combine all ingredients in a heavy saucepan and place over medium-high heat. Bring to a boil, then simmer on medium heat for about 12 minutes or until thickened, stirring occasionally. Let cool.

Yogurt and Caper Dressing

¼ cup (60 mL) fat-free plain yogurt
¼ cup (60 mL) low-fat mayonnaise
1 tsp (5 mL) chopped capers

Whisk ingredients together.

SALMON CAKES

Blomidon Inn, Wolfville, NS

Chef Sean Laceby says that fresh ingredients always give the best results. He also says it is important to put the breadcrumb coating on at the last minute, just before frying: "This really helps to give a crisp exterior and to keep the flavour at its best." This is one of the inn's most popular dishes.

12 oz (340 g) boneless fillets salmon
1 cup (250 mL) mashed potatoes
   (½ lb / 225 g)
1 egg, lightly beaten
¼ cup (50 mL) sour cream
½ cup (125 mL) fresh breadcrumbs
1 tbsp (15 mL) fresh dill
2 tsp (10 mL) salt
1 tsp (5 mL) pepper
For breading:
½ cup (125 mL) fresh breadcrumbs
For cooking:
vegetable oil

Bring a saucepan or deep skillet of water to boil; turn heat to medium and place salmon in pan, ensuring water covers fish. Cook until salmon flakes apart easily, drain and let cool.

In a large bowl, combine salmon, potatoes, egg, sour cream, breadcrumbs, dill, salt and pepper.

Mix well and form into patties. Coat with breadcrumbs.

Heat vegetable oil in a skillet over medium heat, add cakes and brown on both sides, turning once.

4 fishcakes / 2 servings

Suggested sauce: Hollandaise Sauce (see page 89)

SALMON FENNEL CAKES

Though fish cakes are usually made with fresh fish loins, use low-sodium canned salmon here to speed up preparation. There are sustainable canned options out there — make sure to read the label carefully and look for 100% wild Pacific salmon. You don't need to remove the bones from canned salmon — the bones are well-cooked, a good source of calcium, and easily mashed, but you can take them out if you like.

1 large potato
1 can (213 g) salmon, drained but with liquid
   reserved
¼ cup (60 mL) chopped green onions (about 4
   green onions)
½ cup (125 mL) diced fennel bulb
3 tbsp (45 mL) fresh fennel leaves
2 tsp (10 mL) Worcestershire sauce
1 tsp (5 mL) mustard powder
2 tbsp (30 mL) light mayonnaise or salad dressing
dash of hot sauce
fresh ground pepper
flour
1½ tbsp (22 mL) canola oil

Wash potato and pierce all over with a fork. Cook in microwave for 6 to 8 minutes, until tender. In a medium bowl, mash salmon and bones (skin removed and discarded).

In a lightly greased non-stick skillet over medium heat, sauté the green onion and diced fennel bulb for 1 to 2 minutes, stirring with a fork, until fennel is slightly tender. Add green onions, fennel, fennel leaves, Worcestershire sauce, mustard powder, mayonnaise or salad dressing, hot sauce and 1 tbsp (15 mL) reserved salmon liquid (if mixture appears dry) to mashed salmon and mix until well combined. Add pepper to taste.

With your hands, form salmon mixture into 12 patties about 3 inches (7.5 cm) in diameter. Dredge each patty in flour to lightly coat each side.

In a larger non-stick skillet over medium-high heat, place ½ tbsp (7 mL) of oil. When oil is hot, add 4 salmon cakes and cook until browned, flip and continue to cook until browned on other side and heated through. Keep finished patties warm while you repeat instructions, using ½ tbsp oil per 4 patties for the remainder.

12 fishcakes / 4 servings

ATLANTIC SALMON CAKES

Chanterelle Inn, North River, St. Anns Bay, NS

Chef Earlene Busch says the hake in this recipe acts as an emulsifier in place of the more traditional use of breadcrumbs or potato. This makes it an excellent choice for gluten-free diets.

5 oz (140 g) hake (or other white fish such as haddock, sustainably harvested)
1 tsp (5 mL) lemon juice
8 oz (225 g) farmed Atlantic salmon fillet, chopped
½ cup (125 mL) diced onions
1 tsp (5 mL) chopped garlic
½ cup (125 mL) diced celery
1 tbsp (15 mL) chopped fresh parsley
1 tsp (5 mL) salt
½ tsp (2 mL) black pepper
For cooking:
2 tbsp (30 mL) butter
2 tbsp (30 mL) olive oil

In a food processor or blender, liquefy hake with lemon juice. In large bowl, combine hake and lemon juice, salmon, onions, garlic, celery, parsley, salt and black pepper.

Form into patties and refrigerate until chilled.

In a non-stick frying pan over medium heat, combine butter and oil. Sauté patties until golden brown on both sides, turning once.

4 fishcakes / 2 servings

Suggested sauce: Lemon Dill Mayo

Basic Mayonnaise (author's recipe)
1 egg yolk
2 tsp (10 mL) white vinegar
1 tsp (5 mL) dry mustard
7 oz (210 mL) canola oil
lemon juice
salt
pepper

Using a blender, a food processor or an electric mixer with whip attachment lets you make fast, easy homemade mayonnaise. It takes a little longer and a strong arm if done by hand, but the results will be worth the effort.

Whip egg yolk, vinegar and mustard. Add oil, drop by drop, whisking constantly until emulsion is formed. You will see mixture begin to thicken and turn pale. Continue adding oil slowly, adding lemon juice when sauce becomes thick.

Season with salt, pepper and lemon juice to taste.

Note: Ensure intact eggs (no cracks) are used for making mayonnaise.

Variations on Basic Mayonnaise

Curry Mango Mayo: Add 1 tbsp (15 mL) curry
paste and ½ cup (125 mL) chopped mango,
including juice.

Lemon Dill Mayo: Add fresh chopped dill and lemon
juice to taste.

COHO SALMON AND BROCCOLI FISHCAKES

*Gaffer's Bistro, Whitehall Country Inn,
Clarenville, NL*

This recipe started out as salmon cakes served with a cheese sauce, but Chef Chris Sheppard feels it is much improved by mixing the cheddar into the patty mixture.

5 oz (140 g) Coho salmon (boneless, skinless fillet)
½ cup (125 mL) broccoli florets, cut small
2 cups (500 mL) mashed potatoes (1 lb / 450 g)
¼ cup (50 mL) grated cheddar cheese
1 tsp (5 mL) salt
1 tsp (5 mL) white pepper
For cooking:
butter

Bring a saucepan or deep skillet of water to boil; turn heat to medium and place salmon in pan, ensuring water covers fish. Cook until salmon flakes apart easily. Drain and let cool.

Bring a pot of water to boil, plunge broccoli in for about 5 seconds, remove from water and immediately put broccoli into bowl of ice water. Cool and drain well.*

In a large bowl, combine salmon, potatoes, broccoli, cheese, salt and pepper.

Form into patties.

In a non-stick skillet, melt butter over medium heat until it begins to foam. Lightly brown patties on each side. Transfer patties to baking sheet and finish cooking in 400°F (200°C) oven for 10 to 12 minutes.

6 fishcakes / 3 servings

Suggested sauce: Lemon Herb Butter Sauce (see page 52)

*This is called blanching, and it helps set the colour of vegetables, as well as taking away the raw taste.

CHINOOK SALMON CAKES

Gabrieau's Bistro, Antigonish, NS

Chef Mark Gabrieau thinks of this as a down-home traditional fishcake. It's a very versatile recipe as one can substitute haddock for salmon. He suggests combining the potato and salmon just enough to form a patty.

1 lb (450 g) Chinook salmon fillet
¼ cup (50 mL) butter
1 tsp (5 mL) minced garlic
1 cup (250 mL) diced onions
2 cups (500 mL) mashed potatoes (1 lb / 450 g)
½ cup (125 mL) chopped parsley or chives
1 tsp (5 mL) salt
½ tsp (2 mL) pepper
For cooking:
vegetable oil

Bring a saucepan or deep skillet of water to boil; turn heat to medium and place salmon in pan, ensuring water covers fish. Cook until salmon flakes apart easily, drain and let cool.

Heat butter in a frying pan over medium heat; add garlic and onions and cook, stirring frequently, until lightly browned.

Combine salmon, potatoes, garlic, onions, parsley or chives, salt and pepper in bowl. Form into patties and refrigerate overnight.

Heat oil in a skillet over medium heat, add patties and fry until golden brown on one side, then flip and finish cooking on other side. Remove from pan, pat with paper towels and serve.

8 fishcakes / 4 servings

Suggested sauce: Pommery Mustard Cream

Pommery Mustard Cream (author's recipe)
1 cup (250 mL) whipping cream (35% m.f.)
1 tsp (5 mL) lemon juice
1 tbsp (15 mL) grainy mustard (Pommery)
salt and pepper to taste

Over medium heat in heavy-bottomed saucepan, simmer cream until reduced by one third. Stir in lemon juice and mustard. Remove from heat and serve, or refrigerate for later use.

SMOKED SALMON, POTATO AND PORTOBELLO MUSHROOM CAKES

Duncreigan Country Inn, Mabou Harbour, NS

The flavour of smoked salmon varies from one smokehouse to another; try several local smokehouses to find your favourite. When making fishcakes, "scale the fish first!" advises Chef Charles Mullendore.

2 large portobello mushroom caps
1 tbsp (15 mL) olive oil
1 tsp (5 mL) butter
½ cup (125 mL) diced green onions
1 tbsp (15 mL) fresh chopped basil
1 tbsp (15 mL) fresh chopped thyme
1 tbsp (15 mL) fresh chopped parsley
1 cup (250 mL) mashed potatoes (½ lb / 225 g)
1 tsp (5 mL) salt
1 tsp (5 mL) black pepper
8 oz (225 g) smoked salmon, diced
4 oz (110 g) Mabou cheese,* crumbled
½ cup (125 mL) spinach, cooked and chopped
For cooking:
butter

*Mabou cheese is a local delicacy. Substitute feta if you cannot get Mabou cheese.

Brush mushroom caps with olive oil and grill 10 minutes. Chop and set aside.

In a frying pan, sauté onions in butter until soft. Stir in basil, thyme and parsley, set aside to cool.

In a large bowl combine potatoes, smoked salmon, mushrooms, green onions, basil, thyme, parsley, salt, pepper, cheese and spinach. Form into patties and refrigerate for several hours.

In a large skillet, melt butter over medium heat. Sauté patties until golden brown on each side, turning once.

8 fishcakes / 4 servings

Suggested sauce: Red Pepper Aïoli

Red Pepper Aïoli (author's recipe)
2 egg yolks
1 cup (250 mL) canola oil
1 roasted red pepper, peeled and seeded
1 ripe tomato, cored and seeded
1 clove garlic, minced
½ tsp (2 mL) lemon juice
salt and pepper to taste

In food processor, combine egg yolks and oil to the consistency of mayonnaise. Add red pepper, tomato, garlic and lemon juice. Pulse until smooth.

Season to taste with salt and pepper.

Store in refrigerator.

Note: Ensure intact eggs (no cracks) are used for making mayonnaise.

KETA SALMON CAKES

Sweet Basil Bistro, Halifax, NS

Chef Veinotte serves his salmon cakes with any one of three sauces: curry cream sauce, caper sauce or dill cucumber sauce.

6 oz (170 g) Keta salmon fillets
1 cup (250 mL) mashed potatoes (½ lb / 225 g)
2 tbsp (30 mL) chopped fresh cilantro
1 tsp (5 mL) minced chives
¼ tsp (1 mL) Tabasco sauce
¼ tsp (1 mL) Worcestershire sauce
1 egg
2 tbsp (30 mL) mayonnaise
½ tsp (2 mL) salt
¼ tsp (1 mL) black pepper
For breading:
2 cups (500 mL) plain white fresh breadcrumbs
For cooking:
butter

Bring a saucepan or deep skillet of water to a boil; turn heat to medium and place salmon in pan, ensuring water covers fish. Cook until salmon flakes apart easily, drain and let cool.

In a large bowl, combine potatoes, salmon, cilantro, chives, Tabasco sauce, Worcestershire sauce, egg, mayonnaise, salt and pepper.

Form into patties and roll in breadcrumbs to coat thoroughly.

In a non-stick frying pan, heat butter and fry patties over medium-high heat until golden brown.

4 fishcakes / 2 servings

Suggested sauce: Curry Cream Sauce

Curry Cream Sauce (author's recipe)
1 cup (250 mL) whipping cream (35% m.f.)
1-2 tsp (5-10 mL) mild curry paste
1 tsp (5 mL) lemon juice
OR:
To one recipe of Béchamel Sauce (below), whisk in
1 to 2 tbsp (5 to 10 mL) mild curry paste
¼ cup (50 mL) lemon juice

Over medium heat in a heavy-bottomed saucepan, simmer cream (if using) until reduced by one third. Stir in curry paste and lemon juice. Remove from heat and serve, or refrigerate for later use.

Béchamel Sauce (author's recipe)

The classic white sauce, béchamel is versatile and can take on many different seasonings.

4 oz (115 g) clarified butter*
4 oz (115 g) flour
4 cups (1 L) milk, hot
1 small whole onion, peeled
1 whole clove
1 small bay leaf
salt
white pepper
nutmeg

Heat butter in heavy saucepan over low heat. Add flour, stirring to make roux. Gradually add milk, whisking constantly.

Bring sauce to boil, whisking, then reduce heat to simmer.

Stick bay leaf to onion with clove and add to sauce.

Simmer for 30 minutes, stirring occasionally.

Season very lightly with salt, white pepper and nutmeg.

Strain to remove onion.

Sauce may be used immediately, or refrigerated and reheated for later use.

*To clarify butter, heat unsalted butter slowly in heavy saucepan. The milk solids will separate and sink to the bottom. Skim foam off top, carefully pour off the liquid, which is your clarified butter (also known as drawn butter), and discard the solids. Because the milk solid has been removed, clarified butter can be heated to a higher temperature before burning, making it ideal for pan-frying. 2½ lbs (1 kg) of butter will yield 2 lbs (900 g) clarified butter.

LOBSTER

With today's lobster prices, it's hard to believe that in many fishing communities lobster was once considered a poor man's food. When buying live lobster, hold your choice out of the water; the tail should flap or curl under the body and not dangle listlessly. The best way to cook lobster is by plunging it live headfirst into heavily salted boiling water. If this doesn't appeal to you, ask your fish purveyor to cook it for you. Atlantic lobster can be found on the west coast but at exorbitant prices; crab may be used in place of lobster with equally good results in these recipes.

Atlantic lobster has been certified by MSC. SeaChoice has assessed the species as Some Concerns, due largely to a decrease in stocks in specific areas, particularly the Northumberland Strait. However, this is a fishery with open and closed seasons, minimum size limits on catches and protection placed on egg-bearing females, resulting in increased stock productivity in other areas, like southwestern Nova Scotia. All Atlantic lobster are trap-caught, a fishing method with minimal habitat effects and low levels of bycatch.

For more information on SeaChoice's ranking of lobster, please refer to the introduction on page 6.

CHIPOTLE LIME LOBSTER CAKES

Garrison House Inn, Annapolis Royal, NS

Chipotle peppers were traditionally smoked in clay pots in a fire pit. Modern methods of curing the peppers gives them a fuller, mellower flavour that rounds out the palate rather than shocking the taste buds with a sudden heat.

1 lb (450 g) Atlantic lobster meat
1 egg
1 tbsp (15 mL) lime juice
1 tsp (5 mL) chipotle peppers*
1 cup (250 mL) fresh breadcrumbs
1 tsp (5 mL) garlic powder
2 tbsp (30 mL) mayonnaise
1 tsp (5 mL) chopped fresh cilantro
For cooking:
olive oil

In a large bowl, combine all ingredients and form into patties.

In a large skillet, heat oil over medium heat. Sauté patties until golden brown on each side, turning once.

4 fishcakes / 2 servings

Suggested sauce: Cucumber Raita

*Chipotles are dried, smoked jalapenos. They can be usually be found in the Mexican food section. Substitute chili paste if unavailable. When mincing chipotles or any hot peppers, wear gloves and remove seeds and membrane carefully before chopping — the seeds contain most of the "heat." Contact with the bare skin can result in painful burning.

Cucumber Raita (author's recipe)
1 English cucumber
½ cup (125 mL) plain yogurt
1 tsp (5 mL) chopped fresh mint

Peel and seed cucumber. Dice into small cubes. In bowl, mix cucumber, yogurt and mint. Serve chilled.

CHILLED ATLANTIC LOBSTER SALAD CAKES

Le Crocodile, Vancouver, BC

This very light lobster cake should gently fall apart at the touch of a fork. By cooking the potatoes with the skins on, enough starch is retained to allow the cakes to hold their shape. Be sure to use red potatoes.

1 lb (450 g) red-skinned potatoes (about 10 medium-small potatoes)
8 stalks young asparagus
12 red radishes
1 tbsp (15 mL) finely chopped onions
8 oz (225 g) Atlantic lobster meat
½ tsp (2 mL) salt
¼ tsp (1 mL) pepper
1 tbsp (15 mL) lemon juice
2 tbsp (30 mL) Dijon mustard vinaigrette* (or other vinaigrette)

*Dijon Mustard Vinaigrette: 1 part oil to 3 parts vinegar, 1 tsp Dijon mustard (or more to taste).

Boil potatoes until easily pierced with knife. Set aside to cool, then mince.

Cook asparagus in boiling water, cool in ice water. Slice thinly.

Slice radishes thinly.

In a mixing bowl, combine potatoes, asparagus, radishes, onions, lobster, salt, pepper and lemon juice. Toss in vinaigrette.

Mold in small plastic or metal rings, let chill and unmold.

4 fishcakes / 2 servings

LOBSTER CROQUETTES

ela!, Halifax, NS

Chef Joseph says these lobster croquettes were inspired by another favourite served at the restaurant, a dish of chicken stuffed with lobster, scallops and shrimps, accented with lime zest and juice, and finished with a rich wine cream sauce. He adds that citrus zest adds a lot to almost any dish.

¼ cup (50 mL) butter
1 cup (250 mL) diced onions
2 cups (500 mL) mashed potatoes (1 lb / 450 g)
12 oz (340 g) Atlantic lobster meat
12 oz (340 g) baby Northern shrimp
1 tsp (5 mL) orange zest
1 tsp (5 mL) orange juice
1 tsp (5 mL) fresh chopped thyme
3 tsp (15 mL) fresh chopped parsley
2 egg yolks
¼ cup (50 mL) fresh breadcrumbs

¼ tsp (1 mL) black pepper
½ tsp (2 mL) salt
For breading:
1 cup (250 mL) flour
2 eggs, beaten
2 cups (500 mL) fresh breadcrumbs
For cooking:
vegetable oil

Melt butter in frying pan and sauté onions until softened but not browned.

In large bowl, combine mashed potatoes, onions (with butter), lobster meat, baby shrimp, orange zest and juice, thyme, parsley, egg yolks, ¼ cup (50 mL) breadcrumbs, salt and pepper.

Mix thoroughly. Form into patties.

Set up breading station with 3 bowls: first flour, then egg mixture, then breadcrumbs. Dip patties in flour, shake off excess; dip in egg mixture then coat in breadcrumbs.

Cook patties in vegetable oil until browned.

5 fishcakes / 2 to 3 servings

Suggested sauce: Béarnaise Sauce

Béarnaise Sauce (author's recipe)
½ cup (125 mL) white wine vinegar
2 tbsp (30 mL) chopped shallots
2 tsp (10 mL) chopped fresh tarragon
1 tsp (5 mL) pepper
6 egg yolks
1 lb (450 g) warm clarified butter (see page 27)
lemon juice
salt
pepper

Combine vinegar, shallots, tarragon and pepper in a saucepan and reduce by three quarters. Remove from heat and allow to cool slightly.

Transfer to a stainless steel bowl.

Add egg yolks to bowl and beat well using wire whisk.

Hold bowl over a hot water bath (double boiler) and continue to beat mixture until thick and creamy.

Remove bowl from heat. Slowly beat in warm, clarified butter, adding drop by drop at first.

If the sauce becomes too thick, beat in a little lemon juice.

When all butter has been added, season with salt and pepper to taste.

Serve immediately.

SHRIMP & SCALLOPS

Enormously popular and versatile, shrimp is harvested on both east and west coasts. Jumbo shrimp are commonly called prawns on the west coast, although this is a misnomer as the prawn is actually a separate species. The smaller, colder-water species tend to be the sweetest and most flavourful. Shrimp is widely available fresh, frozen and canned; cooked and uncooked; shell on and shell off — take your pick. While there are slight differences in taste and texture, all sizes work well for fishcakes.

SeaChoice has assessed Atlantic trap-caught shrimp and Pacific spot prawn (also trap-caught) as Best Choice, while Atlantic trawl-caught shrimp have Some Concerns due to habitat damage caused by otter trawls. Both fishing methods for Atlantic shrimp have been certified as sustainable by MSC, while the Pacific spot prawn has not been certified.

Scallops are generally grouped in two classes: the tiny bay scallop and the larger sea scallop. As they deteriorate rapidly once harvested, it's rare to see fresh scallops in their shells. Look for creamy or pinkish-tinged flesh that is shiny and has a sweet odour.

Farmed scallops are available from both the Atlantic and Pacific regions, and wild scallops are fished from Atlantic waters. SeaChoice recommends farmed suspended-culture scallops as the best choice of these options. Farmed dredged scallops have been assessed as Some Concerns because of the habitat damage that can arise from dredging. MSC has not assessed farmed scallops because they do not certify aquaculture species at the present time. Wild scallops (also dredged) are assessed as a species to avoid by SeaChoice. Wild scallops harvested from specific fishing areas have been certified by MSC, because they tend to be less critical of the types of fishing gear used.

For more information on SeaChoice's ranking of scallops, and MSC certification, please refer to the introduction on page 6.

ASIAN SEAFOOD CAKES

Dundee Arms Inn, Charlottetown, PE

Chef Patrick Young prepared this recipe with good health in mind: this mixture of seafood has a high content of Omega 3 fatty acids. He has been experimenting with Asian influences in his cuisine for many years.

2 oz (55 g) bay scallops
2 oz (55 g) Northern shrimp
2 oz (55 g) haddock
2 oz (55 g) wild Pacific salmon
1 cup (250 mL) mashed potatoes (½ lb / 225 g)
1 cup (250 mL) cooked Japanese white rice*
   (short grain or sticky)
¼ cup (50 mL) diced carrots
¼ cup (50 mL) diced bell peppers (red, green
   and/or yellow)
¼ cup (50 mL) diced red onions
¼ tsp (1 mL) diced garlic
¼ tsp (1 mL) diced shallots
1 tsp (5 mL) white sesame seeds
1 tsp (5 mL) black sesame seeds
⅛ cup (25 mL) sesame oil
¼ cup (50 mL) soy sauce
1 egg
2 tsp (125 mL) fresh breadcrumbs
For cooking:
vegetable oil

*Arborio, the Italian short grain rice, may be used if you have trouble locating the short grain or sticky Japanese rice.

Dice or chop seafood into small pieces. Bring a pot of water to simmer, place fish in pot and cook until done. Cool and set aside.

In a large bowl, combine seafood, potatoes, rice, carrots, peppers, red onions, garlic, shallots, black and white sesame seeds, sesame oil, soy sauce, egg and breadcrumbs. (The mixture will be fairly wet.) Form into patties.

Pan-fry in vegetable oil over medium-high heat, 4 to 5 minutes each side.

7 fishcakes / 3 to 4 servings

Suggested sauce: Wasabi Cream Sauce

Wasabi Cream Sauce
1 tbsp (15 mL) butter
¼ tsp (1 mL) minced shallots
¼ tsp (1 mL) minced garlic
½ cup (125 mL) dry white wine
2 cups (500 mL) whipping cream (35% m.f.)
1 tsp (5 mL) wasabi powder

In a frying pan over medium heat, sauté shallots and garlic in butter until browning starts. Add white wine, stirring with whisk, and cook a few minutes until wine has almost evaporated. Add cream and cook, stirring occasionally, until sauce begins to thicken.

Stir in wasabi powder and serve.

CRAB

There are several species of crab referred to in these recipes, from the east coast's snow or queen crab to the Dungeness and king crabs on the Pacific side. All crab types may be used interchangeably in crab cake recipes, so go with whatever's fresh and in season.

When buying live crab, look for active specimens and avoid those that appear sluggish or aren't moving. If you're squeamish about throwing live crustaceans in the cooking pot, ask your fish purveyor to do it for you. For convenience, there is high quality, shelled, frozen product available year round. When buying lump crab meat, pick through it carefully for shell fragments.

Pacific Dungeness crab, Jonah crab and Atlantic snow crab are the common Canadian varieties available. SeaChoice's Best Choice recommendation is given to Pacific Dungeness crab, while Jonah and Atlantic snow crab are both assessed as Some Concerns. The concerns in both cases are related to levels of bycatch associated with the fishing methods used. There have been rare incidents of protected marine mammals becoming entangled in trap lines within the Jonah crab fishery, which is a high conservation concern. In the Atlantic snow crab fishery, there are concerns with bycatch of undersized and soft-shelled crabs. None of the three species have been MSC certified.

For more information on SeaChoice's recommendations and MSC certification, refer to the introduction on page 6.

CRAB CAKES

Eagle's Eye Restaurant, Golden, BC

This recipe calls for any white fish. Chef Dave Knoop's first choice is halibut, which complements the crab and offers a light, flaky texture to the dish. Other alternatives include monkfish and jackfish, which have a mild flavour.

7 oz (200 g) haddock or halibut (or other white fish)
11 oz (300 g) crab meat
2 eggs
1 tbsp (15 mL) fresh dill
½ tsp (2 mL) salt
¼ tsp (1 mL) pepper
1 tbsp (15 mL) fresh lemon juice
fresh breadcrumbs

Bring a saucepan or deep skillet of water to boil; turn heat to medium and place fish in pan, ensuring water completely covers it. Cook until well done and flakes apart easily. Remove any bones. Combine fish with all other ingredients.

Form into patties, adding breadcrumbs if mixture is too moist.

Sauté patties in butter until brown on both sides, turning once.

6 fishcakes / 3 servings

Suggested sauce: Pommery Mustard Cream (see page 24)

CRAB CAKES DE BOUCTOUCHE

Auberge Le Vieux Presbytère Restaurant, Bouctouche, NB

Baking powder gives a lightness to this moist cake.

1 lb (450 g) crab meat, drained
1 cup (250 mL) fresh breadcrumbs
⅓ cup (75 mL) milk
¼ cup (50 mL) mayonnaise
1 egg
2 tbsp (30 mL) finely chopped green onions
1 tbsp (15 mL) chopped fresh parsley
½ tsp (2 mL) baking powder
½ tsp (2 mL) salt
¼ tsp (1 mL) white pepper
For cooking:
2 tbsp (30 mL) vegetable oil
2 tbsp (30 mL) butter
flour

Place crab meat in a large bowl. Cover with breadcrumbs and pour milk on top. In a separate bowl, combine mayonnaise, egg, green onions, parsley, baking powder, salt and pepper. Pour over crab mixture and gently toss until mixed.

Form into patties and refrigerate for at least 1 hour.

Heat butter with oil in a large skillet over medium heat.

Dust cakes lightly with flour and fry until golden brown, about 4 minutes each side.

4 fishcakes / 2 servings

Suggested sauce: Lemon Herb Butter Sauce

Lemon Herb Butter Sauce
¾ cup (175 mL) dry white wine
1 tbsp (15 mL) lemon juice
½ tsp (10 mL) chopped shallots
¾ cup (175 mL) whipped cream (35% m.f.)
1 cup (250 mL) unsalted butter, cubed
¼ cup (60 mL) fresh chopped herbs (such as
   parsley or tarragon)
salt and black pepper to taste

Put white wine, lemon juice and shallots in saucepan over medium-high heat. Cook until wine is nearly evaporated. Stir in cream and continue cooking for another 5 minutes.

Turn heat down to medium and begin dropping in butter cubes slowly, one at a time, whisking each one into the sauce. After all butter has been added, remove from heat, add herbs, then salt and pepper to taste and serve immediately

CREAM CHEESE CRAB CAKES

Boffins Club, Saskatoon, SK

The sweet crab flavour and creamy cheese centre of these cakes make a delicious first course. For a luncheon dish or main-course entrée, just add a salad and warm crusty bread.

¼ cup (60 mL) finely chopped red bell pepper
¼ cup (60 mL) finely sliced green onion
¼ cup (60 mL) finely sliced celery
1 tbsp (15 mL) fresh lemon juice
1 tbsp (15 mL) jalapeño hot sauce, or to taste
8 oz (250 g) whipped cream cheese, room
    temperature
1 cup (250 mL) fine bread crumbs
½ tsp (2 mL) thyme
½ tsp (2 mL) basil
pinch of salt
pinch of pepper
1 lb (450 g) lump crabmeat
2 to 3 tbsp (30 to 45 mL) butter
fresh herbs

In a skillet over medium heat, sauté pepper, onion, celery, lemon juice and pepper sauce until the vegetables wilt, about 5 minutes.

Remove from heat and stir in whipped cream cheese until combined. Set aside. In a bowl, combine bread crumbs, thyme, basil, salt and pepper. Set aside. Clean and check crab for shell and cartilage; squeeze gently to remove excess liquid. Cup your hand and place about 2 tbsp (30 mL) of the crabmeat into it. With a blunt knife, spread about 2 tbsp (30 mL) of the cream cheese mixture over the crabmeat. Add another 2 tbsp (30 mL) of the crabmeat, press down and form into a ball. Roll the ball in the crumb mixture until well coated. Place ball on a cutting board and press lightly to form a cake about ¾-inch (2-cm) thick. Repeat process to form 12 crabcakes. Heat butter in a skillet over medium heat. Add crab cakes, being careful not to crowd, and sauté until golden on both sides. To serve, arrange 2 or 3 cakes on each serving plate, drizzle with Creole Mustard Sauce and garnish with fresh herbs.

12 crab cakes / 4 to 6 servings

Suggested sauce: Creole Mustard Sauce

Creole Mustard Sauce
3 tbsp (45 mL) pepper jelly
¼ cup (60 mL) fresh orange juice
¼ cup (60 mL) Creole mustard

In a small saucepan over low heat, combine pepper jelly, orange juice and mustard; stir until sauce consistency. Serve warm.

NORI-WRAPPED CRAB CAKES WITH LEMONGRASS CREAM

Oritalia, Vancouver, BC

Sweet fresh Pacific Dungeness crab blends well with the slightly salty strips of sushi nori that wrap these delectable crab cakes. Add to this the unique lemon-ginger flavour of Chef Julian Bond's Lemongrass Cream sauce and you have an appetizer or luncheon dish that will leave guests in awe. Garnish servings as desired with fresh herbs, edible flowers or enoki mushrooms.

1 lb (450 g) Dungeness crabmeat
3 green onions, chopped
1 clove garlic, crushed
4 tbsp (60 mL) Habañero Mayonnaise (recipe follows)
1 tbsp (15 mL) granulated sugar
1 tbsp (15 mL) lime juice
1 tsp (5 mL) coarsely ground pepper
1 egg, lightly beaten (optional to moisten)
3 sheets sushi nori*
egg wash (1 beaten egg + ½ tsp water)
½ cup (125 mL) all-purpose flour
2 cups (500 mL) bread crumbs
vegetable oil

*Sheets of dried seaweed are available in the specialty section of some supermarkets and in Asian markets.

Clean and check crab for shell and cartilage: squeeze to remove excess liquid. In a bowl, combine crab, green onions, garlic, Habañero Mayonnaise, sugar, lime juice, pepper, and enough egg to moisten (if desired). Using about 3 tbsp mixture per crab cake, form into circles. Cut sushi nori strips to width of circles and attach, moistening ends with some of the egg wash to seal. Coat open sides of circles with flour; dip in remaining egg wash, then bread crumbs. In a skillet, heat ½ inch oil over medium-high heat; fry crab cakes, turning once, for 5 to 7 minutes or until cooked through and light golden. Remove with slotted spatula and drain on paper towels. To serve, creatively arrange crab cakes and Lemongrass Cream on individual dishes with garnish of choice.

12 crab cakes / 4 to 6 servings.

Suggested sauce: Lemongrass Cream

Habañero Mayonnaise

Use this hot mayonnaise as a dressing for sandwiches or as a dipping sauce. It can be refrigerated for up to 4 days. Remember not to touch your eyes when handling Habañero chilis as they will burn. Wash hands thoroughly after dicing. All ingredients should be at room temperature before combining.

1 egg
¼ cup (60 mL) olive oil
1 tbsp (15 mL) lime juice
1 tbsp (15 mL) finely diced seeded Habañero chili pepper
¼ cup (50 mL) vegetable oil
salt

In food processor, beat egg; with machine running, slowly add olive oil in thin steady stream. When mixture begins to thicken, blend in lime juice and Habañero chili pepper. With machine running, slowly add vegetable oil, increasing the flow as mayonnaise thickens and pales. Season with salt to taste.

Makes ¾ cup.

Lemongrass Cream

1 tsp (5 mL) vegetable oil
¼ onion, diced
¼ sweet yellow pepper, diced
1 clove garlic, minced
⅓ cup (80 mL) white wine
3 tbsp (45 mL) lemon juice
1 stalk lemongrass, cut in 2-inch (5-cm) lengths and crushed
¼ cup (60 mL) crushed gingerroot
1 cup (250 mL) (35% m.f.) cream
½ cup (125 mL) mashed potato
1 tbsp (15 mL) liquid honey
salt and white pepper

In a saucepan, heat oil over medium-low heat; sweat onion, yellow pepper and garlic until vegetables are softened. Increase heat to medium; deglaze pan with wine and lemon juice. Enclose lemongrass and ginger in cheesecloth bag; add to sauce along with cream and potato. Reduce by half. Remove cheesecloth bag, squeezing to extract juices. Add honey to sauce, season with salt and pepper to taste. In food processor, purée sauce; strain through fine-mesh sieve.

BAY OF FUNDY CAKES

Dufferin Inn, Saint John, NB

Chef Axel Begner developed this recipe to reflect the inn's location on the shores of the Bay of Fundy. He uses very fresh shellfish — lobster, crab and scallops — and sometimes salmon. His partner Margaret says the cakes should be prepared and served the same day, otherwise they will not hold their shape.

½ lb (225 g) crab meat
½ lb (225 g) lobster meat
½ lb (225 g) scallops
4 tbsp (60 mL) chopped green onions
2 tsp (10 mL) diced shallots
2 tsp (10 mL) diced garlic
1 tbsp (15 mL) chopped fresh dill
1 tbsp (15 mL) chopped fresh parsley
2 tbsp (30 mL) chopped capers
¼ cup (50 mL) mayonnaise
1 tsp (5 mL) salt
½ tsp (2 mL) pepper
3 tbsp (45 mL) fresh breadcrumbs
1 tbsp (15 mL) lemon juice
4 egg yolks
For cooking:
olive oil

In a large bowl, combine all ingredients except olive oil. Form into patties.

Heat olive oil in a skillet over medium-high heat. Brown patties on both sides, then place in 350°F (180°C) oven for 15 minutes until heated through.

7 fishcakes / 3 to 4 servings

Suggested sauce: Moosehead Beer Sauce

Moosehead Beer Sauce
6 egg yolks
1 bottle Moosehead Dry beer (or other dry ale)
1 tbsp (15 mL) maple syrup
¼ tsp (1 mL) salt
¼ tsp (1 mL) pepper
1 tbsp (15 mL) lemon juice

In a large stainless steel bowl, whisk together egg yolks, beer, maple syrup, salt, pepper and lemon juice. Hold bowl over a pot of boiling water and keep whisking until sauce is thick and creamy.

DUNGENESS CRAB CAKES

Catch Restaurant, Calgary, AB

Chef Andrew Hewson advises that you should
use just enough of the scallop mousse to bind the
cakes. Any extra scallop mousse can be rolled
in plastic wrap (like a cigar) and poached. It
can be used as a garnish or as an hors d'oeuvre
topping.

Mousse:
3 oz (80 g) scallops
pinch salt and pepper
1 egg yolk
3 tbsp (45 mL) whipping cream (35% m.f.)

Patties:
1 tbsp (15 mL) butter
1 tbsp (15 mL) finely diced onions
1 tbsp (15 mL) finely diced leeks
1 tbsp (15 mL) finely diced fennel
2 tbsp (30 mL) finely diced red pepper
1 lb (450 g) Dungeness crab meat
1 tbsp (15 mL) chopped parsley
2 tsp (10 mL) chopped cilantro
½ tsp (2 mL) salt
½ tsp (2 mL) paprika
¼ tsp (1 mL) pepper
¼ tsp (1 mL) cayenne pepper

For breading:
1 cup (250 mL) panko breadcrumbs
1 tsp (5 mL) finely chopped orange zest
1 tsp (5 mL) finely chopped lemon zest
1 tsp (5 mL) finely chopped lime zest
1 tsp (5 mL) chopped fresh parsley
For cooking:
vegetable oil

In a food processor, purée scallops with a pinch
of salt and a shake of pepper. Scrape down
sides of bowl and add egg yolk, puréeing
30 seconds. Scrape down sides of bowl.
With processor running, slowly pour in cream.
Refrigerate mousse until ready to use.

In a skillet over medium heat, melt butter and
gently cook onions, leeks, fennel and red peppers
until vegetables are tender but not browned. Set
aside to cool.

In a large mixing bowl, combine cooled
vegetables with crab meat, parsley, cilantro, salt,
paprika, pepper, and cayenne pepper. Form into
patties and refrigerate until chilled.

In a small bowl, combine panko breadcrumbs,
orange, lemon and lime zests and parsley. Coat
patties with breading mixture. Sauté in vegetable
oil over medium-high heat until golden brown on
both sides, turning once.

4 fishcakes / 2 servings

Suggested sauce: Mango Chutney

Mango Chutney
7 tbsp (100 mL) rice wine vinegar
⅓ cup (80 mL) sugar
4 tsp (20 mL) ginger, peeled and chopped fine
2 tsp (10 mL) shallot, chopped fine
1 tsp (5 mL) mustard seed
1 ripe mango, peeled and diced
1 tsp (5 mL) cilantro, chopped

In a small pot, combine rice wine vinegar, sugar,
ginger, shallot and mustard seed and reduce to
syrup consistency.

Add mango and cook 3 to 5 minutes. Strain
liquid from mango and return to pot to reduce
back down to syrup.

Add mango back to the syrup and let cool, stir in
cilantro. Keep in refrigerator for up to 2 weeks.

DUNGENESS CRAB CAKES

Mahle House, Nanaimo, BC

Chef Maureen Loucks makes stunning seafood towers for her unsuspecting guests. First splash a little scallion oil and red pepper purée on the plate. "Throw it down on the plate and it splatters wildly," she advises. Place a dab of the aïoli sauce on the plate followed by the crab cake, add another dab of aïoli to the top of the cake and place a grilled scallop to top it all off. Place two tiger prawns on the side.

1 tsp (5 mL) butter
1 cup (250 mL) finely diced red peppers
1½ lb (675 g) fresh Dungeness crab meat
1 tbsp (15 mL) fresh chopped chives
½ cup (125 mL) panko breadcrumbs
½ cup (125 mL) mayonnaise
For breading:
3 eggs
1 cup (250 mL) panko breadcrumbs
For cooking:
butter
vegetable oil

Heat butter and cook red pepper gently until softened. Set aside and let cool.

In a large bowl, combine crab, chives, red peppers, ½ cup (125 mL) breadcrumbs and mayonnaise.

Form into patties and refrigerate at least 1 hour or overnight.

In a small bowl, whisk eggs. Dip patties in egg, then in 1 cup (250 mL) breadcrumbs.

In a non-stick pan over medium-high heat, melt butter and add oil. Sauté patties until golden brown on both sides, turning once.

6 fishcakes / 3 servings

Suggested sauce: Saffron Aïoli

Saffron Aïoli (author's recipe)
3 or 4 saffron strands
¼ cup (50 mL) dry white wine
2 egg yolks
1 cup (250 mL) canola oil
1 clove garlic, minced
salt and pepper to taste

Soak saffron strands in wine to bring out colour.

Whisk egg yolks in a small bowl. Add oil drop by drop, gradually increasing flow to thin stream until mixture thickens.

Add garlic, wine-saffron mix and seasonings to taste.

CRAB CAKES

Seasons Restaurant, Vancouver, BC

These crab cakes make a great lunch with the rémoulade and a few mixed greens. For another version of the dish, try panko (Japanese breadcrumbs) instead of regular breadcrumbs and change the sauce to a lime ginger aïoli with a small amount of soya and sesame oil.

½ lb (225 g) crab meat
¼ cup (50 mL) very finely diced red pepper
¼ cup (50 mL) very finely diced celery
¼ cup (50 mL) very finely diced red onion
3 tbsp (45 mL) diced chives
1 cup (250 mL) fine breadcrumbs
1 cup (250 mL) mayonnaise
1 tbsp (15 mL) dry mustard
¼ tsp (1 mL) Tabasco sauce
⅛ tsp (½ mL) Worcestershire sauce
1 tbsp (15 mL) lemon juice
⅛ tsp (½ mL) cayenne pepper
salt and pepper to taste
For cooking:
canola oil

In a large bowl, combine crab, red pepper, celery, onion, chives and breadcrumbs.

In a second bowl, stir together mayonnaise, mustard, Tabasco sauce, Worcestershire sauce, lemon juice, cayenne, salt and pepper.

Fold crab mixture into seasoned mayonnaise. Form into patties and refrigerate until chilled.

Sauté patties over medium-high heat until browned on both sides, turning once.

4 fishcakes / 2 servings

Suggested sauce: Cajun Rémoulade (see page 70)

POTATO CRAB CAKES

Shaw's Hotel, Brackley Beach, PE

The combination of diced celery, red pepper and parsley creates a very colourful crab cake. The rich flavour comes from adding sour cream.

2 tbsp (30 mL) butter
1 cup (250 mL) finely chopped Spanish onions
½ cup (125 mL) finely chopped celery
¼ cup (50 mL) finely chopped red bell pepper
1 tbsp (15 mL) chopped garlic
2 cups (500 mL) mashed potatoes (1 lb / 450 g)
1 lb (450 g) crab meat
¼ cup (50 mL) chopped green onions (green part only)
¼ cup (50 mL) grated Parmesan cheese
¼ cup (50 mL) chopped flat leaf (Italian) parsley
2 tbsp (30 mL) lemon juice
1 tbsp (15 mL) salt
¾ cup (175 mL) dried fine breadcrumbs
¼ cup (50 mL) sour cream
Seasoned flour mixture:
¼ cup (50 mL) flour
2 tbsp (30 mL) salt
1 tbsp (15 mL) garlic powder
2 tbsp (30 mL) black pepper
1 tbsp (15 mL) onion powder
2 tbsp (30 mL) dried dill
For breading:
2 eggs
1 tbsp (15 mL) water
¾ cup (175 mL) dried fine breadcrumbs
For cooking:
vegetable oil

In a small pan, melt butter over medium heat. Add onions, celery, bell peppers and garlic, cooking until softened but not browned. Remove from heat and set aside.

In a large bowl, combine potatoes, crab meat, green onions, Parmesan, parsley and lemon juice. Add cooled onions, celery, bell peppers and garlic. Add salt and breadcrumbs. Fold in sour cream.

Form into patties and refrigerate.

In a separate bowl, prepare the seasoned flour: combine flour, salt, garlic powder, black pepper, onion powder and dried dill.

In another bowl, whisk eggs and water.

Set up breading station with 3 bowls: first seasoned flour, then egg mixture, then breadcrumbs. Dip the patties in flour, shake off excess; dip in egg mixture, then coat in breadcrumbs.

In a large skillet, heat oil over medium heat. Sauté patties until golden brown on each side, turning once.

10 fishcakes / 5 servings

Suggested sauce: Lemon Dill Mayonnaise
(see page 21)

POTATO-CRUSTED SNOW CRAB CAKES

Chives Canadian Bistro, Halifax, NS

Chef Darren Lewis says, "This recipe is an original; the crust doesn't come from the traditional breadcrumbs. It is made from potato flakes. We have the luxury of living close to the ocean. The crab comes directly from the shores of Cape Breton or northern New Brunswick."

2 tbsp (30 mL) butter
½ cup (125 mL) diced red onions
½ cup (125 mL) diced celery
1 lb (450 g) snow crab leg meat
1 cup (250 mL) fresh breadcrumbs
½ cup (125 mL) diced red peppers
2 egg yolks

¼ cup (50 mL) chopped chives
½ tsp (2 mL) hot pepper sauce
1 tsp (5 mL) Worcestershire sauce
1 1/2 tsp (7 mL) salt
1 tsp (5 mL) pepper
For breading:
1 cup (250 mL) flour
3 egg yolks
¼ cup (50 mL) buttermilk
1 cup (250 mL) potato flakes
For cooking:
vegetable oil

Melt butter in a skillet over medium heat; cook red onions and celery until softened but not browned. In a large bowl, combine crab, breadcrumbs, red onions, red peppers, celery, 2 egg yolks, chives, hot pepper sauce, Worcestershire sauce, salt and pepper in bowl. Form into patties and refrigerate until well chilled.

Mix 3 egg yolks and buttermilk. Set up breading station with 3 bowls: first flour, then egg yolk mixture, then potato flakes. Dip cakes in flour, shake off excess; dip in egg yolk mixture, then coat in potato flakes.

Deep-fry cakes at 350°F (180°C) until golden brown.

5 fishcakes / 2 to 3 servings

Serving suggestions: Chives' Sour Cream, Pickled Red Onions

Chives' Sour Cream

1 cup (250 mL) sour cream
1 tbsp (15 mL) prepared horseradish
1 tbsp (15 mL) grainy Dijon mustard
1 tbsp (15 mL) minced shallots
¼ cup (60 mL) chopped chives
salt and fresh cracked pepper to taste

Combine all ingredients and let stand refrigerated overnight for best flavour.

Pickled Red Onions

1 large red onion
1 cup (250 mL) red wine vinegar
1 cup (250 mL) brown sugar
2 tbsp (30 mL) sea salt
1 tbsp (15 mL) black pepper
1 bay leaf
1 tbsp (15 mL) grenadine (for colour; optional)

Slice onion, separate into rings and set aside in glass container.

In saucepan, bring red wine vinegar, brown sugar, sea salt, black pepper, bay leaf and grenadine to boil.

Pour boiling mixture over onions in glass container, making sure onions are completely submersed in liquid.

Refrigerate overnight.

Drain and serve onions as garnish or side dish.

THAI CRAB CAKES

RainCoast Café, Tofino, BC

Bean sprouts give a bit of crunch to these cakes, both inside and out. RainCoast owner Lisa Henderson mentions that for a similar effect you can substitute daikon — a white radish. Oyster sauce adds depth and a hint of sweetness to the crab cakes.

2 lbs (900 g) cooked halibut (or other white fish)
1 lb (450 g) crab meat
1¼ cups (300 mL) panko breadcrumbs
1 cup (250 mL) fresh bean sprouts, coarsely chopped
¼ cup (50 mL) finely chopped green onions
¼ cup (50 mL) finely chopped fresh cilantro
2 tbsp (30 mL) fresh lime juice
⅛ tsp (0.5 mL) red pepper flakes
1 tsp (5 mL) oyster sauce
1 large egg
For cooking:
canola oil

In a large mixing bowl, combine fish, crab, breadcrumbs, bean sprouts, green onions, cilantro, lime juice, red pepper flakes, oyster sauce and egg. Mix well, form into patties and refrigerate for several hours.

Sauté patties in canola oil over medium-high heat until golden brown on both sides, turning once.

8 fishcakes / 4 servings

Suggested sauce: Lemon Aïoli (see page 93)

HADDOCK & SABLEFISH

In addition to cod, there are many kinds of white fish available. The most popular are haddock and halibut. Sablefish, lingcod and hake are also good choices. These are all mild-tasting fish and can be substituted one for another.

When buying whole fish, look for shiny scales and bright eyes. If the fish is already filleted, check for smell — there shouldn't be a strong fishy aroma. To get the best fish, find a reliable source with high turnover and knowledgeable staff. Buy fresh in season. When buying frozen, beware of signs of freezer burn or frost in the package.

In the Atlantic haddock fishery, two fishing methods are commonly used: hook-and-line, and trawl. SeaChoice has assessed the hook-and-line fishery to be less damaging to the marine ecosystem, and has recommended hook-and-line haddock as the Best Choice, while trawl-caught haddock should be avoided. MSC has certified both hook-and-line and trawl-caught haddock with certain conditions placed on each fishery.

Pacific sablefish is fished using traps or bottom longline, and is assessed as SeaChoice's Best Choice. This species is also MSC certified.

Halibut is fished from both the Atlantic and Pacific using bottom longline. Pacific halibut is the only species of halibut that has been certified as sustainable by the MSC. SeaChoice has some concerns with this species because of the amount of bycatch, which is now being monitored. Atlantic halibut is only fished from the Scotian Shelf and South Grand Banks, where stocks are low but seem to be stabilizing.

For more detailed information on haddock, halibut and sablefish, regarding the SeaChoice evaluation and MSC certification, please see the introduction on page 6.

SEAFOOD CAKES

Marshlands Inn, Sackville, NB

Chef Roger says these cakes can be made thick for a main course, or thinner to serve as an appetizer. If you find the cakes too crumbly, he suggests adding another egg and more breadcrumbs to bind the seafood.

4 oz (115 g) Chinese noodles (or rice vermicelli)
4 oz (115 g) haddock
1 oz (30 g) scallops
1 oz (30 g) shrimp
8 tsp (40 mL) chopped green onions
3 tbsp (45 mL) butter
2 oz (60 g) lobster meat
½ cup (125 mL) grated Asiago cheese
1 tsp (5 mL) salt
1 tsp (5 mL) pepper
2 tbsp (30 mL) fresh parsley
½ cup (125 mL) fresh breadcrumbs
2 eggs
For cooking:
vegetable oil

Cook noodles until tender. Rinse and chop into 2-inch pieces. Set aside.

Sauté haddock, scallops, shrimp and green onions in butter until just cooked. Add lobster to seafood mixture and let cool.

In large bowl, combine seafood and green onions, noodles, cheese, salt, pepper, parsley, breadcrumbs and eggs.

Form into patties.

In a non-stick pan over medium-high heat, cook patties in oil until golden brown on both sides.

4 fishcakes / 2 servings

Suggested sauce: Jalapeño Jelly

Jalapeño Jelly
¼ cup (50 mL) chopped fresh jalapeños*
¾ cup (175 mL) chopped red pepper
1 cup (250 mL) white vinegar
3 tbsp (45 mL) lemon juice
5 cups (1250 mL) white sugar
6 oz (170 g) Certo (fruit pectin)

Wearing gloves, slice jalapeños in half lengthwise and scrape out seeds. In blender, process jalapeños, red pepper and ½ cup (125 mL) vinegar until smooth. Pour into a saucepan; add remaining vinegar, lemon juice, sugar and Certo. Bring to boil and cook 10 minutes. Remove from heat and skim.

Cool and store in Mason jars.

*If fresh jalapeños are unavailable, use ¼ cup (50 mL) chopped canned jalapeños.

SMOKED LINE-CAUGHT HADDOCK CAKES WITH SWEET CORN AND TARTAR SAUCE

Chives Canadian Bistro, Halifax, NS

This is no ordinary fishcake and no ordinary tartar sauce. The smoky haddock and sweet corn work perfectly together and the crunchy and slightly acidic condiment finish it off beautifully. Chef Craig Flinn smokes his own fresh haddock and purchase line-caught whenever possible. However, there are many very good smokehouses that make a great smoked haddock, so pick some up if you can. Smoked mackerel or hotsmoked salmon make very good substitutes here.

4 tbsp (60 mL) minced red onion
4 tbsp (60 mL) minced celery
4 tbsp (60 mL) minced red pepper
1 clove garlic, minced
1 cup (250 mL) fresh kernel corn
3 tbsp (45 mL) salted butter
1 tsp (5 mL) salt
1½ lb (675 g) smoked haddock
1 medium potato, cooked and grated
½ cup (125 mL) fresh breadcrumbs
1 cup (250 mL) mayonnaise
1 tsp (5 mL) Tabasco or hot sauce
1 tsp (5 mL) Worcestershire sauce
2 tbsp (30 mL) chopped green onion tops or chives

For breading:
3 eggs
¼ tsp (1 mL) salt
¼ tsp (1 mL) pepper
½ cup (125 mL) flour
1½ cups (375 mL) panko or regular dried breadcrumbs
¼ cup (60 mL) vegetable oil

Sweat red onion, celery, red pepper, garlic and corn in butter and salt until onions are translucent. In a large mixing bowl, flake haddock into small pieces using your fingers. Add grated potato, fresh breadcrumbs, sweated vegetables, mayonnaise, Tabasco sauce, Worcestershire sauce and green onions and mix thoroughly using your hands. Form into patties and chill in refrigerator for a minimum of 1 hour before breading.

In a small mixing bowl, beat eggs with salt and pepper. Dredge fishcakes first in flour, then eggwash and finally breadcrumbs. Heat vegetable oil in a nonstick frying pan and fry breaded fishcakes over medium heat until crisp and golden, about 6 minutes per side.

Serve with a heaping spoonful of tartar sauce and garnish with herbs or microgreens.

8 fishcakes / 4 servings

Suggested sauce: Tartar Sauce

Tartar Sauce
3 tbsp (45 mL) minced Pickled Red Onions (see
    page 73), or fresh red onion
2 tbsp (30 mL) finely chopped capers
¼ cup (60 mL) diced gherkins
1 tbsp (30 mL) sweet green relish
1 cup (250 mL) mayonnaise
¼ cup (60 mL) sour cream
1 tsp (5 mL) Tabasco sauce
1 tsp (5 mL) Worcestershire sauce
juice and zest of 1 lemon
½ tsp (2 mL) salt
¼ tsp (1 mL) freshly ground black pepper
2 tbsp (30 mL) chopped chives, optional

Combine all ingredients in a small mixing bowl and stir well. Store in a sealed container, refrigerated, for up to 10 days.

SMOKED SABLEFISH CAKES

Metropolitan Hotel, Vancouver, BC

Chef Baechler explains that cooked sablefish
has a light buttery flavour and flaky texture which
is similar to sea bass. Sablefish is flash-frozen
immediately on the boats to preserve freshness.
"Nothing beats fresh fish," says the chef, "but with
this freezing technique, you can hardly taste the
difference." He suggests making the fishcakes the
morning before you serve them and chilling them
in the refrigerator.

2 cups (500 mL) warm mashed potatoes
   (1 lb / 455 g)
½ lb (225 g) cooked flaked smoked sablefish
1 tbsp (15 mL) chopped fresh cilantro
1 tbsp (15 mL) chopped fresh chives
1 tbsp (15 mL) butter, melted
salt
pepper
lemon juice
For breading:
1 egg
3 tbsp (45 mL) cold water
1 cup (250 mL) panko breadcrumbs
For cooking:
olive oil

In a large mixing bowl, combine potatoes, fish,
cilantro, chives and butter; season with salt,
pepper and lemon juice to taste.

Form into patties and refrigerate for at least 1
hour.

Whisk egg with cold water in a bowl. Gently dip
patties, one by one, in the egg mixture, then coat
well with breadcrumbs.

In a shallow non-stick pan, lightly brown patties in
olive oil on medium heat.

6 fishcakes / 3 servings

Suggested sauce: Red and Green Tomato Salsa

Red and Green Tomato Salsa
1 tsp (5 mL) olive oil
½ sweet red pepper, diced
½ fresh jalapeño pepper, seeded and diced (see
   page 30)
2 plum tomatoes, seeded and diced
3 small green tomatoes, seeded and diced
⅓ cup (80mL) chopped fresh coriander
¼ tsp (1 mL) ground coriander
1 tbsp (5 mL) lime juice
1 tsp (5 mL) hot pepper sauce
salt and pepper to taste

Gently toss all ingredients in large glass bowl,
refrigerate and allow flavours to blend, up to
4 hours.

SMOKED HOOK-AND-LINE HADDOCK FISHCAKES WITH CELERY ROOT, APPLE AND GOLDEN BEET SALAD

Five Fishermen, Halifax, NS

Fishcakes are a very personal item, and many people claim to make the best version. Fishcakes are comforting cold-weather food, sometimes served with baked beans for a weekend supper. They make great morning brunch with eggs over easy and green tomato chow, or as Renée Lavallée presents them here, a lovely lunch or appetizer with a unique coleslaw-inspired salad. You could use any fish for a fishcake but smoked haddock is a great choice for flavour and aroma. The white truffle oil Renée uses is available at nearly any good grocery store or international food market and will keep for a long time in the fridge.

1 lb (450 g) smoked haddock
1 lb (450 g) baby red-skinned or
   yellow-fleshed potatoes
1 tsp (5 mL) sea salt
several grindings of black pepper
juice and zest of 1 lemon
3 tbsp (45 mL) extra-virgin olive oil
½ cup (125 mL) grated Parmesan cheese
4 tbsp (60 mL) chopped fresh tarragon
1 tsp (5 mL) white truffle oil
½ cup (125 mL) canola oil
1 cup (250 mL) panko breadcrumbs (Japanese-style)

Flake smoked haddock and set aside. Steam or boil potatoes until cooked. Place still-warm potatoes in a stand mixer with paddle and crush slightly, making sure not to overprocess. Add flaked haddock, salt, pepper, lemon juice and zest and mix to combine. Add olive oil while mixing on slow speed until mixture starts to stick together. Add Parmesan, tarragon and truffle oil. Taste for seasoning and add more if you feel that it is needed.

Using an ice cream scoop (2 oz / 60 g), form fish mixture into cakes. Pour canola oil into frying pan and place over high heat. Quickly dip cakes into panko crumbs and place in pan. Cook on one side for 1½ minutes, until golden brown, then flip over. Cook for an additional minute, and remove from oil. Place onto a baking tray and into a preheated 400°F (200°C) oven to finish for 3 to 4 minutes.

Serve fishcakes with a large spoonful of salad.

12 fishcakes / 6 servings

Celery Root, Apple and Golden Beet Salad

1 small celery root, peeled and julienned
1 firm, tart apple (such as Honeycrisp or
  Jonagold), peeled and julienned
1 golden beet, peeled and julienned
juice and zest of ½ lemon
1 tsp (5 mL) honey
½ cup (125 mL) chopped flatleaf parsley
¼ cup (60 mL) extra-virgin olive oil
salt and pepper to taste

Mix celery root, apple and beet in a bowl. In
a separate bowl, mix together lemon juice and
zest, honey, parsley, olive oil and seasonings.
Combine with vegetables, mix and marinate for 1
hour before serving.

DUNGENESS CRAB AND SABLEFISH CAKES

Kingfisher Resort and Spa, Courtenay, BC

26 oz (750 g) Dungeness crab meat
11 oz (300 g) sablefish fillet, cooked
3 tbsp (45 mL) chopped green onion
¼ cup (50 mL) diced sweet red pepper
2 tbsp (30 mL) mayonnaise
1 egg
For breading:
2 tsp (10 mL) black pepper
1 tsp (5 mL) chili pepper flakes
1 tbsp (15 mL) lemon zest
½ tsp (2 mL) sea salt
1 cup (250 mL) flour
¼ cup (50 mL) cornmeal
2 eggs
2 tsp (10 mL) lemon juice
1 tsp (5 mL) Worcestershire sauce
2 cups (500 mL) panko breadcrumbs
For cooking:
2 tbsp (30 mL) olive oil
3 tbsp (45 mL) butter

In a large mixing bowl, combine crab meat, sablefish, onions, red pepper, mayonnaise and 1 egg. Form into patties and refrigerate for at least 1 hour.

In a spice grinder or clean coffee mill, grind black pepper, chili pepper flakes, lemon zest and sea salt. Add spice mix to flour and cornmeal in a bowl.

In a bowl, whisk 2 eggs with lemon juice and Worcestershire sauce. Set up breading station with 3 bowls: first flour, then egg mixture, then breadcrumbs. Dip patties in flour, shake off excess; dip in egg mixture, then coat in breadcrumbs.

In a non-stick skillet over medium heat, melt butter and oil. Sauté patties until golden brown on both sides, turning once.

10 fishcakes / 5 servings

Suggested sauce: Lemon Aïoli (see page 93)

FISH-LEEK CAKES

Hillcroft Café and Guest House, Lunenburg, NS

Don't skip the pungent Thai fish sauce; it adds a
subtle flavour that makes these cakes unique.

1 lb (455 g) haddock fillets
2 cups (500 mL) mashed potatoes (1 lb/455 g)
¼ cup (50 mL) melted butter
2 cups (500 mL) finely sliced leeks*
2 eggs
1 tbsp (15 mL) Thai fish sauce
2 tsp (10 mL) finely chopped parsley
1 tsp (5 mL) paprika
½ tsp (2 mL) cayenne pepper
1 tsp (5 mL) salt
½ tsp (2 mL) black pepper

For breading:
3 eggs
2 tbsp (30 mL) vegetable oil
1 cup (250 mL) flour
1 cup (250 mL) fresh breadcrumbs
1 cup (250 mL) cornmeal
For cooking:
vegetable oil

*To prepare leeks for cooking, split lengthwise
in quarters and spread layers apart to wash
thoroughly. We use both the white and green
parts.

Bring a saucepan or deep skillet of water to a boil; turn heat to medium and place haddock in pan, ensuring water covers fish. Cook until haddock is well done and flakes apart easily. Set aside to cool.

Sauté leeks in melted butter until softened but not brown. Set aside.

In a large bowl, combine fish, potatoes, leeks, butter, 2 eggs, Thai fish sauce, parsley, paprika, cayenne, salt and pepper.

Form into patties and refrigerate until well chilled.

Beat 3 eggs with oil. Combine cornmeal and breadcrumbs. Dredge patties in flour, then egg wash, then cornmeal / breadcrumb mixture.

Heat oil in large skillet over medium heat. Add fishcakes (oil should come halfway up the sides of the cakes). Fry until both sides are golden, drain on paper towels.

10 fishcakes / 5 servings

Suggested sauce: Hollandaise Sauce

Hollandaise Sauce *(author's recipe)*
¼ tsp (1 mL) salt
¼ tsp (1 mL) pepper
3 tbsp (45 mL) white vinegar (or white wine
   vinegar)
2 tbsp (30 mL) cold water
16 egg yolks
1 lb (455 g) warm clarified butter (see page 17)
2 tbsp (30 mL) lemon juice

Combine salt, pepper and vinegar in saucepan and reduce until nearly dry. Remove from heat and add cold water.

Transfer to a stainless steel bowl. Add egg yolks, and beat well using wire whisk.

Hold the bowl over a hot water bath (double boiler) and continue to beat yolks until thick and creamy.

Remove the bowl from heat. Slowly beat in the warm clarified butter, adding butter drop by drop at first.

If the sauce becomes too thick, beat in a little lemon juice.

When all butter has been added, add remaining lemon juice.

Taste and add more salt and pepper if you like. Serve immediately.

CHIVES' FISHCAKES WITH SPINACH SAUCE

Chives Canadian Bistro, Halifax, NS

This recipe uses small bits of nearly any type of fish. If you make any seafood dish, simply save the trim and perhaps buy an extra tailpiece from your fishmonger. The next day — fishcakes! Planning meals like this is a great way to save money and time, as you can often prep dishes two at a time.

3 lb (1.4 kg) fish trim
3 tbsp (45 mL) butter or olive oil
¼ cup (60 mL) minced red onion
¼ cup (60 mL) minced fennel bulb
½ tsp (3 mL) fennel seed, toasted and ground
2 green onions, finely chopped
3 tbsp (45 mL) chopped fresh parsley
⅓ cup plus 1 tbsp (100 mL) mayonnaise
¼ cup (60 mL) dry breadcrumbs
1 sprig fresh tarragon, chopped
juice and zest of half a lemon
½ tsp (3 mL) salt
½ tsp (3 mL) freshly ground black pepper
1 tsp (5 mL) Tabasco sauce
For breading:
1 cup (250 mL) flour
3 eggs, beaten
1½ cups (375 mL) dry breadcrumbs, preferably panko
2 cups (500 mL) vegetable oil (for pan-frying)

Place the fish trim on a baking tray, spread in an even layer. Bake the fish in a 350°F (180°C) oven for about 7 or 8 minutes, just until the fish is opaque and barely cooked. It should still look juicy and be slightly firm to the touch. Allow the fish to cool to room temperature, then gently flake the fish with your fingers into a large mixing bowl.

In a sauté pan, cook the red onions, fennel and fennel seed in the butter or oil until just translucent, about 4 minutes. Add the sautéed vegetables to the mixing bowl containing the fish, then add all the remaining ingredients to the fish and mix very well with your hands. Portion the mixture into 8 equal piles and form them into cakes roughly the size of a hockey puck. Refrigerate the cakes for at least 1 hour before breading.

Place the flour, eggs, and breadcrumbs in 3 separate containers on the counter and remove the fishcakes from the fridge. Roll each cake first in the flour, patting it gently with your hands to remove any excess flour. Dip the cake next in the beaten eggs (known as an eggwash), and finally, the breadcrumbs. The breadcrumbs should stick nicely to the cakes if you follow this procedure.

Heat the vegetable oil in a steep-sided pan to 350°F (180°C). You can also use a household deep-fryer for this step, should you own one. If so, follow the instructions and heat the oil to "high." Carefully fry the cakes in the oil until golden brown on both sides. When frying the cakes in a shallow pan with less oil, flip them after 3 or 4 minutes on each side. The cakes can be held in a 250°F (120°C) oven until ready to serve.

To serve the cakes, ladle 2 ounces of spinach sauce in the center of a warm plate. Place the fishcake in the center of the pool of sauce and garnish with your favourite pickle or a small side green salad.

8 fishcakes / 8 servings

Suggested sauce: Spinach Sauce

Spinach Sauce
½ cup (125 mL) white wine
2 tbsp (30 mL) white wine vinegar
2 tbsp (30 mL) shallots, finely chopped
1 bay leaf
6 white peppercorns
1 cup (250 mL) heavy cream (35% m.f.)
1 cup (250 mL) vegetable stock
10 oz (320 g) spinach, washed
juice and zest of half a lemon
several grindings of black pepper
⅛ tsp (½ mL) celery salt

Combine wine, vinegar, shallots, bay leaf, and peppercorns in a saucepan over medium heat; reduce by half. Add the cream and stock and reduce again by half. Place the spinach in a blender, add the hot cream mixture, and purée. Add the lemon juice, lemon zest, pepper, and celery salt. Strain the sauce through a fine-meshed strainer (optional). Pour sauce into a saucepan and set aside until you are ready to serve the fishcakes, then reheat over medium-high heat just until warmed through.

SMOKED SABLEFISH CAKES

Café Brio, Victoria, BC

Sablefish is the Canadian term for black cod. The high fat content gives these fish more flavour than other white fish. They are ideal for smoking.

4 cups (1 L) mashed Yukon Gold potatoes
  (2 lbs / 900 g)
½ cup (125 mL) unsalted butter
1 tsp (5 mL) minced garlic
½ cup (125 mL) whipping cream (35% m.f.)
3 sprigs fresh thyme
8 oz (225 g) naturally smoked sablefish (black
  cod)
1 egg yolk
1 tsp (5 mL) salt
1 tsp (5 mL) pepper
For breading:
2 eggs
½ cup (125 mL) milk
1 cup (250 mL) flour
2 cups (500 mL) fresh breadcrumbs
For cooking:
vegetable oil

In a large skillet, heat butter. Sauté garlic until soft, add cream, thyme and sablefish and simmer until fish begins to fall apart. Remove from heat and remove thyme stems and any fish bones. Strain and reserve liquid.

In a large bowl, combine fish and potatoes. Pour in enough of reserved liquid to bring mixture together. Add egg yolk, salt and pepper.

Form into patties and refrigerate until cool.

Whisk eggs and milk.

Set up breading station with 3 bowls: first flour, then egg mixture, then breadcrumbs. Dip patties in flour, shake off excess; dip in egg mixture then coat in breadcrumbs.

In a heavy skillet, heat vegetable oil. Sauté patties over medium heat until golden brown.

10 fishcakes / 5 servings

Suggested sauce: Lemon Aïoli

Lemon Aïoli

1 egg yolk

1 tsp (5 mL) Dijon mustard

½ clove garlic, chopped

1 tsp (5 mL) chopped capers

2 tsp (10 mL) lemon zest

¾ cup (180 mL) canola oil

3 tbsp (45 mL) lemon juice

4 tsp (20 mL) chopped fresh dill

½ tsp (3 mL) Tabasco sauce

½ tsp (3 mL) salt

¼ tsp (1 mL) white pepper

In a large stainless steel bowl, whisk egg yolk, Dijon mustard, garlic, chopped capers and lemon zest.

While whisking, very slowly drizzle in canola oil. As the aïoli thickens, alternate oil with lemon juice until oil and juice have been all incorporated.

Add chopped dill, Tabasco sauce, salt and white pepper.

INDEX

PHOTO CREDITS

Photography by Jen Partridge, Partridge Photography with the following exceptions:

Hamid Attie Photography: 76; Julian Beveridge: 34, 72; Meghan Collins: 21, 24, 30, 35, 52, 68, 87; iStock: 6, 7, 8, 9, 12, 28, 33, 36, 44, 53, 65, 83; Janet Kimber: 18, 27; Scott Munn: 23, 25, 32, 60, 61, 69, 75, 88, 93